in asso(

p

C000027058

The world premiere

31 HOURS

by Kieran Knowles

First performance at the Bunker Theatre: Tuesday, 3 October 2017.

31 HOURS
by Kieran Knowles

CAST IN ORDER OF SPEAKING

John	Abdul Salis
Ste	James Wallwork
Neil	Salvatore D'Aquilla
Doug	Jack Sunderland

The action takes place on a Tuesday morning somewhere on the railways.

The performance lasts approximately eighty minutes. There is no interval.

PRODUCTION TEAM

Director	Abigail Graham
Designer	Andrew D Edwards
Lighting Designer	Sally Ferguson
Sound Designer	Adrienne Quartly
Casting Consultant	Sophie Parrott CDG
Production Manager	Anoushka Hughes-Lewis
Stage Manager	Rachel Graham
Producer	Annabel Williamson
Work gear provided by	Arco®

CAST

Abdul Salis John

Theatre includes *Barbershop Chronicles* (National Theatre), *Birth!* (Manchester Royal Exchange), *Boy* (Almeida), *The Initiate*, *Lungs* and *My Teacher's a Troll* (Paines Plough), *The Rise and Shine of Comrade Fiasco* (Gate), *Henry V* (Unicorn), *War Horse* (National Theatre/New London), *Joe Guy* (New Wolsey/ Soho), *Don Juan in Soho* (Donmar) and *Exonerated* (Riverside Studios/Dublin Festival).

Television includes *Power Monkeys*, *Doctors*, *Hacks*, *Strike Back*, *Outnumbered*, *Victoria Wood Christmas Special*, *Casualty*, *MI High*, *The Bill* and *Doctor Who*.

Film includes *Trendy*, *Flyboys*, *Animal*, *Sahara*, *Welcome Home* and *Love Actually*.

James Wallwork Ste

James trained at the London Academy of Music and Dramatic Art.

Theatre includes *Operation Crucible* (Sheffield Crucible/Finborough/UK tour), *Last Man Standing* (Nursery Theatre), *Darkness* (Edinburgh Festival/Lakeside Colchester) and *My Beautiful Laundrette* (ATS Theatre).

Television includes *Casualty* and *Doctors*.

Film includes *The High Window*, *Nightstand*, *V.P* and *A Thousand Empty Glasses*.

Salvatore D'Aquilla Neil

Salvatore trained at the London Academy of Music and Dramatic Art.

Theatre includes *Operation Crucible* (Sheffield Crucible/Finborough/UK tour), *War Horse* (National Theatre/New London) and *The Way of the World* (Chichester Festival Theatre).

Television includes *Doctors*.

Jack Sunderland Doug

Jack trained at the London Academy of Music and Dramatic Art.

Theatre includes *punkplay* (Southwark Playhouse).

Film includes *Boogieman*.

PRODUCTION TEAM

Kieran Knowles Playwright

Kieran trained at Loughborough University and the London Academy of Music and Dramatic Art, and completed the Royal Court Young Writers Programme. He is co-artistic director of From Ground Up Theatre Company and has recently started a project for unrepresented actors called *(RE)PRESENTED*. His debut play *Operation Crucible* was first performed at the Finborough Theatre before transferring to the Sheffield Crucible and touring with House.

He is currently adapting the play for BBC Radio Four and is under commission from Sheffield Crucible.

Abigail Graham Director

Abigail is artistic director of OpenWorks Theatre.

Work as a director for OpenWorks includes *And Now: The World!* (OpenWorks and Company of Angels in association with Derby Theatre, UK tour) and *Debris* (OpenWorks, Southwark Playhouse).

Theatre includes *Death of a Salesman* (Royal & Derngate), *Man v Dog* (National Theatre Studio), *Timmy Failure: Mistakes Were Made* (Assembly Rooms, Edinburgh), *Molly Sweeney* (Print Room, Lyric Belfast, Northern Irish tour), *The Censor* (JMK runner up, Young Vic workshop performance), *Blue Heaven* (Finborough), *Jack's Quest* (Company of Angels Theatre Maker Award) and *The Boy and the Dog Who Walked to the Moon* (Pleasance, Edinburgh).

Directing in community and education includes *Lines in the Sand* (Derby Playhouse), *Days of Significance* (Royal & Derngate), *Write Now* (Synergy, HMP Send), *One Act Play Festival* (Almeida), *The Ward Project* (Young Vic at Maudsley Hospital), *Remember How to Fly* (Young Vic SEN Festival), *Soft Scoop* (Clean Break) and *The Bridge Project* (Almeida).

As associate director theatre includes *Enron* (Chichester/Royal Court), *Ruined* (Almeida), *Glass Menagerie* (Young Vic), *Wallenstein* (Chichester), *Death and the Maiden* (West End) and *Great Expectations* (Bristol Old Vic).

Andrew D Edwards Designer

Andrew trained at Wimbledon School of Art.

Jerwood Young Designer at the Gate and a finalist for the Linbury Biennial Prize for Design.

Theatre includes *William Wordsworth* (ETT/Theatre by the Lake), *Labyrinth and Donny's Brain* (Hampstead), *Plaques and Tangles* and *Who Cares* (Royal Court), *Romeo and Juliet* (Shakespeare's Globe/World tour), *As You Like It* (Shakespeare's Globe), *The House of Bernada Alba* (La Comédie-Française), *Love's Labour's Lost* (Madrid), *Miss Julie/Black Comedy* (Chichester Minerva Theatre),

Running Wild and *The Hundred and One Dalmatians* (Chichester Festival Theatre), *Blue Remembered Hills*, *Playhouse Creatures* and *Fred's Diner* (Chichester Festival Theatre/Theatre on the Fly), *Impossible* (West End/International tour), *Five Finger Exercise* and *The Dumb Waiter* (Print Room), *The Life and Times of Fanny Hill* (Bristol Old Vic), *Les Parents Terribles* (Donmar Season at Trafalgar Studios), *Backbeat* (West End/Toronto/Los Angeles), *A Voyage Around my Father* (Salisbury Playhouse), *Measure for Measure* (Theatre Royal Plymouth/UK tour), *Jesus Christ Superstar* (Madrid/European tour), *Single Spies*, *Heroes*, *Educating Rita* and *Lettice and Lovage* (Watermill Theatre) and *Quiz Show* (Traverse).

Forthcoming credits include *Après la Pluie* (Théâtre du Vieux-Colombier, Comedie Française, Paris) and *Fack ju Göhte* (Werk 7, Munich).

Opera includes *Così Fan Tutte* (Central City Opera) and *La Bohéme* (Opera Holland Park).

Sally Ferguson Lighting Designer

Theatre includes *While We're Here* (Up In Arms), *The Two Boroughs Project* (Young Vic), *Sweet Charity* (Manchester Royal Exchange), *Jess and Joe Forever* (Orange Tree/Farnham Maltings), *We Wait In Joyful Hope*, *And Then Come The Nightjars* and *Many Moons* (Theatre503), *Big Fish* (Arts Ed Studio Theatre), *Shiver* and *Lost in Yonkers* (Watford Palace), *The Sleeping Beauties* (Sherman Cymru), *Hag*, *Microcosm* and *The Girl With The Iron Claws* (Soho), *Floyd Collins* (Southwark Playhouse), *Slowly* (Riverside Studios), *The Imagination Museum* (UK touring dance production), *Cosi Fan Tutti* (Village Underground), *The Devils Festival* (Print Room) *Devils: Dan Ayling*, *Petra Jean Phillipson*, *Hurbert Essakow* and *The Marriage of Figaro* (Wiltons Music Hall/Musique Cordial, Sellians), *The Wonder!*

A Woman keeps a Secret (BAC), *Christie In Love* and *African Gothic* (The White Bear), *Saraband* (Jermyn Street Theatre), *Trying* (Finborough), *Medea* (Platform Theatre), *Little Me* and *Fiddler On The Roof* (Bridewell/NYT), *Shoot/Get Treasure/Repeat* and *Eschara* (Northcott Exeter), *No One See The Video* (The Rosemary Branch) and *Whisper* (The Place/Lindbury Studio, Royal Opera House).

Co-design includes *As You Like It* (Southwark Playhouse).

Dance includes *The Edge Of Words* and *The Drowner* (The Place), *Subtext: Black Market Tale Traders* (Cargo) and *Story Whores* (Southwark Playhouse/Paper, Scissors, Stone).

Other work as an associate lighting designer includes *The Magic Flute* (Teatro Campoamor, Oviedo), *Street Scene* (Theatre Du Chatelet, Paris/Gran Teatre de Liceu, Barcelona/UK tour), *The Human Comedy* (Young Vic/Watford Palace Theatre), *Richard III* and *Comedy Of Errors* (UK tour), *The Enchanted Pig* (New Victory Theatre, New York/UK tour), *The Lion's Face* (Linbury Studio/Royal Opera House/UK tour), *I Saw Myself* (Jerwood Vanburgh Theatre),

The Corridor (Queen Elizabeth Hall, Southbank Centre/Bregenz Opera House), *One Evening* (Lincoln Centre, New York), *Into Little Hill* (Linbury Studio, Royal Opera House/Gran Teatre de Liceu, Barcelona), *The Shops* (Linbury Studio, Royal Opera House/Bregenz Opera House).

Art Installation: *Kill The Workers* (Chisenhale Gallery, London/Walter Phillips Gallery, Banff & Badischer Kunstverein, Karlsruhe).

Adrienne Quartly Sound Designer

Adrienne trained at the Royal Central School of Speech and Drama.

Theatre includes *Napoleon Disrobed* (Told by an Idiot), *Get Happy* (Beijing Comedy Theatre), *Opening Skinner's Box* (Improbable, New York), *From the Ground Up* (Almeida), *Heroine* (High Tide), *Rose* (Home, Manchester), *The Crucible* (Selladoor/Queen's Theatre, Hornchurch), *A Tale of Two Cities* (Royal & Derngate), *Cuttin' It* (Young Vic/Royal Court), *I Am Thomas* and *365* (National Theatre Scotland), *Bad Jews* (Theatre Royal Haymarket), *Splendour* (Donmar), *A Raisin in the Sun* and *One Monkey Don't Stop No Show* (Eclipse), *Ghost Train*, *Two Clever by Half* and *You Can't Take it with You* (Told by an Idiot/Manchester Royal Exchange), *The Ladykillers* (Newbury Watermill), *After Electra* (Tricycle), *Sex and the Three Day Week* (Liverpool Everyman), *Grand Guignol* (Southwark Playhouse), *Untold Stories* (West Yorkshire Playhouse), *Every Last Trick* (Spymonkey), *My Zinc Bed*, *Private Fears in Public Places*, *Just Between Ourselves* and *Habeas Corpus* (Royal & Derngate), *Inside Wagner's Head* (Linbury, Royal Opera House), *Fräuline Julie* (After August, Barbican/Schaubühne), *Rings of Saturn* (Halle Kalk, Cologne), *Body of an American* and *Tejas Verdes* (Gate), *Here Lies Mary Spindler* (RSC), *The Container* and *The Shawl* (Young Vic), *Stockholm* (Frantic Assembly), *And the Horse You Rode in on* (Barbican Bite Festival), *93.2FM* (Royal Court), *4,000 Miles* (Ustinov, Bath), *The Fastest Clock in the Universe* (Hampstead), *Woyzeck* (St Ann's Warehouse, New York), *The Importance of Being Earnest* (Rose Kingston/Hong Kong Festival), *The Vortex* (Rose Kingston), *Chekov in Hell*, *Horse Piss for Blood*, *The Astronaut's Chair* and *Nostalgia* (Plymouth Drum).

As composer theatre includes *The Whipping Man* (Plymouth Drum), *Lighter than Air* and *3 Little Pigs* (Circo Ridiculoso), *Rumplestiltskin* (Norwich), *Goya* (Gate), *The Tragedy of Thomas Hobbes* (RSC), *Faustus*, *Volpone*, *The Duchess of Malfi* and *School for Scandal* (Stage on Screen).

Anoushka Hughes-Lewis Production Manager

Anoushka trained at the London Academy of Music and Dramatic Art.

Theatre includes *Jam* (Finborough), *The Good Person of Szechwan* (Young Actors Theatre), *7 Rep Directors Showcase* (London

Academy of Music and Dramatic Art), *Love Play* (Young Actors Theatre), *Tape* (The Drayton Arms) and *The Importance of Being Earnest* (Band of Others Productions).

Opera includes *La Italiana de Algeri* (Pop-Up Opera).

Exhibitions and installations include *Art of Make Believe Interactive Exhibition* (National Theatre) and *The Halloween Project* (Stitch in Time Productions).

Rachel Graham Stage Manager

Rachel has a BA (Hons) in Stage Management, Rose Bruford College of Theatre and Performance.

Theatre includes *Some Lovers* (The Other Palace), *Treating Odette* (Upstairs at the Gatehouse), *Lonely Planet* (Tabard), *Jam* (Finborough), *Posh – all female production* (Pleasance Theatre), *Pyjama Game* (Urdang Academy at Pleasance Theatre), *Cinderella* (First Family Entertainment), *Magnificence* (Fat Git Theatre), *Down to Margate* (Joseph Hodges Entertainments), *Sweeney Todd* (Royal Academy of Music) and *Sister Act* (Curtain Call Productions).

W14 Productions Producer

W14 Productions was founded by Annabel Williamson in 2014 with a focus on new writing.

Recent productions include *Jam* (Finborough),*The Brink* (a co-production with the Orange Tree) and *The Late Henry Moss* and *Upper Cut* (Southwark Playhouse).

PRODUCTIONS ACKNOWLEDGEMENTS

31 Hours has been generously supported by The Carne Trust, Arco® and the Campaign Against Living Miserably, CALM.

Thank you also to the British Safety Council, Gate Theatre, London Academy of Music and Dramatic Art, Paines Plough, Southeasten Railway Facilities Department, Swan Films, Young Vic, Ben Deery, Charlotte Dove, Robert Hastie, Tom Hughes, Patrick Knowles, Ben Macintosh, Nick Quinn, Sean Rigby, Wilbur Graham-Hughes CDG and Paul Tinto.

A playground for Ambitious Artists to create work for Adventurous Audiences

The Bunker is an Off-West End theatre in London Bridge that opened in October 2016. Housed in a former underground parking garage, the space was transformed from its original abandoned state into a unique 110-seater deep beneath the pavements of Southwark Street.

With four concrete pillars marking out the performance space, an eclectic mix of audience seating on three sides of a thrust stage, and a snug bar tucked into the corner of the venue, The Bunker has a special character that feels both classical and contemporary at the same time.

Founded by Artistic Director Joshua McTaggart and Executive Producer Joel Fisher, The Bunker's first year of work has included the award-winning sell-out show SKIN A CAT, Cardboard Citizen's 25th Anniversary epic HOME TRUTHS, and most recently the world premiere of dark thriller EYES CLOSED, EARS COVERED.

With ambitious artists at the centre of its programming, The Bunker is proud to be a venue that champions work that pushes beyond convention and expectation for an Off-West End venue.

FIND OUT MORE
Website: www.bunkertheatre.com
Box Office: 0207 234 0486
E-Mail: info@bunkertheatre.com
Address: 53a Southwark Street, London, SE1 1RU

The Bunker Team

Artistic Director Joshua McTaggart
Executive Producer Joel Fisher

General Manager David Ralf
Technical and Theatre Manager Hannah Roza Fisher
Head of Operations Lee Whitelock
Associate Director Sara Joyce
Associate Technical Manager Chris Drohan
Assistant Bar Manager Kevin Bousay

Production Assistant Matthew Turbett

The Bunker could not run smoothly without the incredible work of our volunteer Front of House team. If you would like to join The Bunker team, then email us on **info@bunkertheatre.com**

Our Supporters

The Bunker would like to thank the following supporters:

Howard Panter, Mark Schnebli, Philip and Chris Carne, Laurence Isaacson, The Edwin Fox Foundation, Monty Fisher, Charlotte Houghteling, Joscelyn Fox and Lt Cdr Paul Fletcher, Roger Horrell, Melvyn Dubbell, Quay Chu, Paul Slawson-Price, George Arthur, Roger Horrell, Sara Naudi, Felicity Trew, Edward Glover, Matthew Payne, Alex Leung, Barbara Cantelo. The Stephen Sondheim Society, Matt Brinkler and Max Stafford-Clark.

If you would like to support the work that The Bunker creates, you can find out how at:

www.bunkertheatre.com/support-us

Kieran Knowles

31 HOURS

OBERON BOOKS
LONDON

WWW.OBERONBOOKS.COM

First published in 2017 by Oberon Books Ltd
521 Caledonian Road, London N7 9RH
Tel: +44 (0) 20 7607 3637 / Fax: +44 (0) 20 7607 3629
e-mail: info@oberonbooks.com
www.oberonbooks.com

A catalogue record for this book is available from the British
Library.

PB ISBN: 9781786822819
E ISBN: 9781786822826

Cover photography by Ben Macintosh

Printed and bound by 4EDGE Limited, Hockley, Essex, UK.
eBook conversion by CPI Group (UK) Ltd, Croydon, CR0 4YY.

Visit www.oberonbooks.com to read more about all our books and to buy
them. You will also find features, author interviews and news of any author
events, and you can sign up for e-newsletters so that you're always first to
hear about our new releases.

To those who think no one is listening

At the end of the play the character names which have appeared throughout the narrative are replaced by alphabetical prefixes (A-D). Each of the characters will assume a letter according to a predetermined understanding worked out in rehearsal. It is for a director to decide how they would like to interpret this, however it is my intention that a different character takes their life (performs the role of 'A') in each performance. The randomness and spontaneity in the conclusion of the piece is designed to mirror the unpredictable/instinctive nature of rail suicides. It is my hope that in production each of the characters has been built to a point where they might decide to take their own life, we discover which one in those final passages.

I have removed many of the stage directions, those that remain are merely for context, they are optional and open to interpretation.

The jumps and transitions between scenes can be handled in whatever manner the creative team decide, however, there are a wealth of sounds and lighting opportunities unique to the rail network that would lend themselves to distortion or abbreviation. There is also a 'language' to on-track behaviour outlined by the Rail Safety and Standards Board's (RSSB) documents on Personal Track Safety which would be useful to incorporate and utilise. These are available online.

The play was written in accordance with the Samaritans' Media Guidelines For Reporting Suicide and their Drama Portrayal Factsheet. I have tried to incorporate their advice into the structure of the piece and have been deliberately wary of details and specifics throughout. There are a number of videos on the Samaritans website which offer real life context to the fiction we present here.

If you have been affected by any issues in this piece, I urge you to contact any of the charities listed below:

Samaritans. Email: jo@samaritans.org.uk / Tel: 116 123

Maytree. Email: maytree@maytree.org.uk / Tel: 020 7263 7070

Campaign Against Living Miserably (CALM).
Email: info@thecalmzone.net / Tel: 0800 585858

Or go here: http://www.nhs.uk/Conditions/Suicide/

Train noise builds to a crescendo.

Lights up the four stand in high visibility orange, with blue helmets equipped with head torches, they are inspecting the aftermath of a rail suicide.

It's a Tuesday morning.

Despite its initial appearance, this is not a typical job.

Silence for a long time.

JOHN: Fucking hell.

> *Another long pause.*

* *

STE: "Alright Neil, thanks for coming today, my name is Carl I am the Cleaning Operations Manager, If you get the job, you'll report to me, this is Catherine who works in HR."

JOHN: "Hi."

NEIL: Hello.

STE: "Neil, just to let you know the questions we ask today are standard and were put together by our HR team, they're fairly simple and aren't designed to catch you out."

NEIL: Ok.

STE: "Neil, do you have any questions before we begin?"

NEIL: Err – No.

STE: "Great. Catherine?"

JOHN: "Hi Neil. Nice easy one to start off, what can you tell us about Network Rail?"

DOUG: We work for Network Rail's specialist cleaning branch.

STE: It is our job to attend accidents.

JOHN: Incidents.

STE: Incidents sorry.

DOUG: We are usually the first on site.

STE: Well, sometimes we get there after the police.

JOHN: But we do tend to be amongst the first to…you know.

DOUG: Get our hands dirty.

JOHN: "Anything to add Neil?"

NEIL: No, that's about it.

STE: "Right… Ok, thank you for that…"

NEIL: Oh yeh. Shit. You own all the rail, whatsit. Tracks and buildings and stuff.

STE: "Infrastructure"

NEIL: Yeh, sorry, yeh…forgot to mention that.

STE: "Yep."

NEIL: Sorry, didn't mean to swear.

JOHN: "So Neil, why are you applying for this position?"

DOUG: It's our job to facilitate the transport police.

STE: So that they are able to ascertain identity.

JOHN: And stupid as it sounds, cause of death.

STE: Which is usually being hit bloody hard by a train.

DOUG: It's obviously upsetting at times.

STE: But you can't let it get to you.

JOHN: "Sorry Neil, I didn't catch that."

NEIL: I said I don't know.

JOHN: "You don't know?"

NEIL: I can't think.

JOHN: "Alright."

DOUG: People underestimate the speed –

JOHN: Definitely.

STE: And the size.

JOHN: Yeh.

DOUG: Of the trains.

JOHN: Normally you see a them from a platform –

STE: But –

DOUG: When you're at ground level –

JOHN: It can be towering above you.

DOUG: Twelve feet. Lots of power.

STE: Bodies explode.

JOHN: And blood is a chemical waste.

DOUG: So it's our job to get it cleared up.

NEIL: I mean, I didn't get fired, but I just wanted to leave because the environment was… I saw this on the website and I thought…it was a good opportunity to…it seemed like I would – could, it was like it seemed like I would be good at it.

JOHN: "Thank you Neil."

DOUG: 60 minutes travel and 75 to clean up.

STE: That's the target.

JOHN: If we're more than an hour away.

DOUG: They outsource.

JOHN: Yeh, they get a contractor in.

DOUG: But, that's expensive.

STE: So they don't like doing it.

DOUG: Cheap bastards.

JOHN: From impact to normal service should take about 3 hours.

STE: But it can take a bit longer if you get a 'Popper'.

DOUG: Bloody hell.

JOHN: Don't say that.

STE: What?

DOUG: Sorry about him.

JOHN: He means if the impact is particularly…

DOUG: If someone is hit in a certain way then…

STE: They pop!

JOHN: Jesus Christ.

NEIL: …and I were captain at the time, so I went in there and said you know, you've hit him pretty hard there Timothy, do you know what I'm saying Cath? His name was Timothy, you've gone in a bit rash and the referee has given you a red card, so I think you should leave the field now. Because the referee had just shown him the red, and so what I'm trying to say, you know, I think I was able to calm the situation, you know, but it also shows that I was a good team player because I probably stopped Timmy getting punched in the face.

JOHN: "Thanks Neil, that was actually the last question, so if you don't have anything for us?"

NEIL: No I don't think I do…erm actually…when will I? I mean, when is it that I'll find out?

STE: "Erm…"

* *

DOUG: Ready?

STE: Bag

NEIL: Zip

DOUG: Overalls

STE: Waterproof

DOUG: Radio

STE: Face mask

JOHN: Belt

DOUG: Zip

STE: Pause.

DOUG: My name is Doug, and I'm team leader.

JOHN: He isn't bloody leader.

NEIL: There's no such thing.

JOHN: I'm John.

DOUG: That over there is –

STE: Ste.

DOUG: And this is –

Beat. NEIL isn't looking.

JOHN: Neil, that's Neil.

NEIL: What?

STE: Never mind we've moved on.

DOUG: Deep breath

NEIL: Stop

DOUG: Look

JOHN: Think

DOUG: Assess

STE: Your concerns

NEIL: The risks

DOUG: And feelings

JOHN: How are you feeling?

STE: Fine

JOHN: Great

NEIL: Pause.

JOHN: Discuss

STE: Advise

NEIL: You must

DOUG: Discuss

JOHN: Communicate

STE: Question

DOUG: And advise

NEIL: You must

STE: Prior to

JOHN: Before you

DOUG: Start to

JOHN: Plan

DOUG: Before you start to plan

NEIL: In order to

JOHN: Avoid

STE: Unwanted

DOUG: Injuries

JOHN: Pause.

NEIL: Clear the obvious

JOHN: The visible

DOUG: Clear the obviously visible

STE: The limbs

JOHN: The bones

NEIL: The bodies and the phones

JOHN: The rings

DOUG: And things

NEIL: Clear the other bits of bling

STE: Clear hats

NEIL: And clothes

DOUG: And put it all in rows

STE: So we can tag it

JOHN: And bag it

DOUG: And then bring in the hose

STE: So we can clean

NEIL: And spray

DOUG: And wash it all away

JOHN: The blood

DOUG: The gore

STE: A little piece of jaw

NEIL: And then we scrub

JOHN: We scrub

DOUG: We seriously scrub

STE: Clear the shit

NEIL: And scum

DOUG: Until our hands go numb

JOHN: And then like fighters

STE: Covered in detritus

NEIL: Just our hats to light us

JOHN: We are blowing

DOUG: Adrenaline is flowing

STE: Filth and dirt

DOUG: Exhausted by the hurt.

NEIL: We stop

JOHN: Out of breath

STE: About to flop

NEIL: We stop

DOUG: And it's gone

NEIL: We go

JOHN: A blink

DOUG: A flash

STE: Ago

DOUG: We stop

STE: Bag

NEIL: Zip

STE: Face mask

DOUG: Radio

STE: Waterproof

JOHN: Overalls

NEIL: Belt

DOUG: Zip

STE: Pause.

* *

DOUG: It was a Tuesday.

> I remember that.

> Tuesdays are always the hardest days to get up.

> We were on 'earlys' so it made it even harder.

> It was frosty.

JOHN: I'd heard a rumour.

DOUG: Crisp.

JOHN: About work, nothing serious. But a rumours a rumour.

STE: Cold. It was very cold.

JOHN: And even though you know rumours are just Chinese whispers, they always have a beginning don't they?

STE: Cold…and lonely.

DOUG: I got in the car and drove to the station, parked up, usual spot, it was icy.

JOHN: Someone always has to say something to start one off.

NEIL: It was in the middle of everything else.

JOHN: And when it gets to you, obviously its warped, but someone said something about you.

> You just don't know what.

DOUG: It was strange. I just –

STE: I was thinking. 'I can't be bothered' you know because of the cold.

DOUG: Just had this feeling.

NEIL: Work was an escape. Just – yeh.

STE: I was thinking that.

DOUG: From the moment I woke up…everything felt difficult.

STE: Like a chore.

NEIL: The wife, the baby.

JOHN: And I hate that.

NEIL: Yeh. An escape.

* *

JOHN: "My name is PC Williams, I am with the British Transport Police based out of Crewe. I was called to the scene on the Tuesday morning. Nothing strange about it really.

Unfortunately.

Just another jumper."

DOUG: "Fran Wallace, station manager. I was on call that morning. Still at home.

Still in bed."

JOHN: "The man were middle aged. Again not unusual, it was all very neat.

The driver, a Paul Monroe had reported the incident to the Train Operating Company's switchboard."

DOUG: "My first responsibility is to my staff and my passengers. Fortunately this happened in an area just away from both which is a positive – I suppose.

I just thought – typical, every bloody time I'm on call."

JOHN: "The station manager was on-site and the coroner had been informed.

There was no reason to suspect foul play, though an investigation was opened.

I don't have the case number.

Sorry."

DOUG: "I called the boys, emailed them as well, I didn't know at that point…obviously."

* *

STE: This is a young man

JOHN: He is 34

NEIL: "ish"

JOHN: Called

NEIL: "David"

JOHN: He works in a –

STE: DIY store

JOHN: Thank you, he works in a DIY store as

NEIL: "Deputy Store Manager"

DOUG: £19,995 basic salary

STE: Additionals based on store and team target achievement

JOHN: The targets are not being achieved

NEIL: "Not for some time"

DOUG: And that is putting pressure on –

JOHN: "Me"

STE: This is his wife

JOHN: "Janine"

STE: She has to stay at home because they have a young boy called

NEIL: "Walter"

JOHN: Which puts a lot of pressure on them

NEIL: "Another mouth to feed"

DOUG: Plus

STE: David has credit cards

JOHN: Tah-Dah

DOUG: Loads of them

JOHN: But the straw that breaks the camel's back

DOUG: Is a small

STE: But not insubstantial bout of

DOUG: Depression

NEIL: "Depressed"

DOUG: He is depressed

NEIL: "I am"

JOHN: It's April

DOUG: Raining

NEIL: "Pouring down"

STE: He leaves the house

NEIL: "As normal"

DOUG: He makes his way to the station

STE: And

DOUG: It hits him

STE: He realises

DOUG: This –

STE: It isn't for him

DOUG: It's no fun

JOHN: Not anymore

DOUG: He is no longer having any fun

Neil: "None"

STE: And then the decision

DOUG: Is easy

JOHN: It's not even a decision

NEIL: "It's an instinct"

STE: A reaction

DOUG: A natural progression

JOHN: He doesn't want to hurt anyone

NEIL: "No"

STE: But he can't cope

NEIL: "No"

DOUG: But maybe the kid?

NEIL: "No, he'll be better off"

STE: Maybe the Mrs?

NEIL: "She hates me anyway"

JOHN: How about the mortgage, the debt?

NEIL: "They'll write it off, surely"

STE: Will they?

DOUG: Erm

NEIL: "Surely –"

JOHN: No, you'll still have the debt

NEIL: "I have life insurance"

DOUG: Nope

NEIL: "What?"

STE: Suicide invalidates all insurance

NEIL: "Right"

STE: But to be fair you probably don't know that

NEIL: "Yeh, no, I didn't, I don't, I wouldn't know that"

DOUG: Yeh, that'll be the sort of thing Janine will find out

JOHN: "He's a bastard, he knew he'd leave me like this"

NEIL: "I didn't – Don't –"

JOHN: "I will never forgive him for this"

STE: Bit harsh

NEIL: "No, I just –"

STE: It was easier

JOHN: An option

DOUG: A moment

STE: A question

NEIL: "A chance."

* *

JOHN: I hated it.

I…

Sorry

It's – Erm…

Beat.

I'm coming up on 20 years service.

On the railway.

Beat.

It's all I know.

Beat.

All I –

My life is this job, this job and holidays I can't afford.

That's it.

Beat.

That's it.

So any rumour…

Beat.

Sorry.

Pause.

Sorry.

* *

STE: "Michael Savage, ticket inspector. Conductor. I was working on the train, that day, Tuesday, I was working at the time of the incident."

NEIL: "Paul Monroe."

STE: "I was discussing the route a passenger would have to take when arriving at Crewe in order to continue on to Manchester Piccadilly. Fairly simple."

NEIL: "Train driver."

STE: "I was in the front carriage.

There was a lurch as the brakes were applied and a hard squelchy thud. I knew, instantly."

NEIL: "It's a very lonely time. In the aftermath."

STE: "People were looking out of the windows to either side; they were trying to get a glimpse."

NEIL: "There's obviously phone calls and…but essentially it's you in a small cabin, thinking about what you just saw. What you just did."

Thinking about it, over and over."

STE: "I made contact with the driver via the intercom.

"Was that what I thought?" I asked."

NEIL: ""Yes" it was all I could say.

It's hard. Because all I could think of was the life, the choices which he made to end up in front of the train.

In front of me."

STE: "I couldn't see any blood or claret on the windows so I knew it must have been a fairly clean hit."

NEIL: "This was the first time I'd…you know."

STE: "My job was, essentially, to sit tight, and wait for instructions."

* *

DOUG: John, pass us the juice. John!

JOHN: Sorry?

DOUG: The bleach

JOHN: Here

STE: It's important that you pack everything away clean

DOUG: Otherwise next time you come to use it

STE: It'll be all hard and shitty

NEIL: Right.

DOUG: Grab that broom

NEIL: Right.

DOUG: Dunk it

NEIL: What's that?

DOUG: Water

NEIL: Right.

DOUG: And soap and some disinfectant

NEIL: Right.

DOUG: Then you pull it out

STE: Shake it over a drain

JOHN: Dunk it again

NEIL: Right.

DOUG: See all that blood?

NEIL: Yeh.

STE : Then you pour a bit of bleach on it

JOHN: Leave it for a minute

DOUG: Dunk it again

JOHN: Then pack it away

DOUG: And you do that with everything

NEIL: Right.

STE: Hold these Neil

NEIL: The first month was crazy.

DOUG: Neil, come here

NEIL: I was more of a servant than a colleague.

JOHN: Erm… Sorry lad what's your name?

NEIL: Neil.

STE: Neil, that's it, can you nip back to the station and ask them for the usual?

NEIL: Erm… What's the usual?

STE: Coffee, white, boring

JOHN: Tea – strong.

DOUG: Black –

JOHN: Splash of milk

DOUG: Coffee

JOHN: Semi skimmed

DOUG: Two sugars

NEIL: Right.

JOHN: What are you doing?

NEIL: Sorry?

STE: Neil, I thought you were getting the drinks?

NEIL: I think it was because I was new. I didn't know the routines.

DOUG: Bloody hell

NEIL: The shorthand

JOHN: Take your time Neil

NEIL: It's funny when you start something new, isn't it?
First you have to learn the actual day to day job, then you have to learn the people…what they're like and what they want from you.

STE: Hold these Neil

NEIL: Give us a minute.

DOUG: Neil, come here

NEIL: Why?

DOUG: Because I bloody said so

JOHN: Erm… Sorry lad what's your name?

NEIL: Neil.

STE: Neil?

DOUG: Neil.

JOHN: Neil!

NEIL: Piss off. It's trial and error but you get there in the end.

* *

JOHN: Gasping

STE: Breathing

NEIL: Panting

DOUG: Breath

JOHN: Gasping

STE: Breathing

NEIL: Panting

DOUG: Breath

JOHN: Air

STE: I need –

JOHN: Gasping

STE: Breathing

NEIL: Panting

DOUG: Breath

JOHN: Air

STE: I need air

NEIL: I need

DOUG: Need air

JOHN: Gasping

STE: Breathing

NEIL: Panting

DOUG: Breath

JOHN: Air

DOUG: I Need, I –

STE: I –

NEIL: Need air.

* *

> *STE stands alone.*
>
> *He pulls out a wallet and fishes in it for a picture.*
>
> *He shows it to the audience.*

STE: Hard copy.

I've got more on my phone, but I keep this one with me.

I just –

Yeh.

> *As if feeling he has said too much, he carefully puts the picture away.*

* *

DOUG: "Erm… Jennifer Flowers. I was a passenger on the train.

The police were brilliant.

It was very calm."

NEIL: "Manic. It's always manic."

DOUG: "It was early in the morning, dark. It was still dark. And frosty.

I just felt the braking. And straight away you think, that's not normal, trains don't normally brake like that. Someone fell over. In the aisle."

NEIL: "Sorry, I'm Tina King, I'm a Rail Care Team volunteer. Have been for 7 years.

We are always on call for suicides in our area. We're just there to help. To assist."

DOUG: "Then there was a long pause, we were just sitting there.

Waiting.

It was cold."

NEIL: "We identify passengers who may not be coping, help them, offer them a shoulder. We're the caring side of the company."

DOUG: "No one was speaking. Which isn't unusual I guess, but they weren't listening to anything either. It was just silent. Heavy. It was like we were at a remembrance service for the person already. There were a couple of people walking the train advising us of what had happened, what they were doing, and how long these things can take. They looked sympathetic."

NEIL: "Sometimes they have to isolate the train, which means it loses power, that can shock passengers, being plunged into near darkness."

DOUG: "I just remember the calm, they even dimmed the lights."

JOHN: "Fuming. I was fuming. And everyone was deflecting."

NEIL: "This was my sixteenth suicide. Fourth this year."

STE: "Sir this is a very serious matter."

JOHN: "Said the conductor, who had been breezing up and down the train all morning with an unearned sense of authority. Serious!"

STE: "There are a number of logistical issues as I am sure you'll appreciate."

JOHN: "How can I fucking appreciate them, when we are just sat here, clueless. It is a joke! The lights weren't on, it was pitch black, freezing. The company should have plans for this –"

STE: "I'll stop you there."

JOHN: "What?"

STE: "This is a Network Rail issue."

JOHN: "It was infuriating. Thoughtless prick. How can you do this, kill yourself like this. There's a train full of people here, 400, 500 people, all just trying to get to work, trying to have a normal Tuesday, and one idiot kills himself and now we are all sat here managing the consequences."

STE: "Sir, this is an ongoing situation –"

JOHN: "I don't even have phone service, my phone isn't in service. I was taking photos though. I was going to tweet the shit out of this, taking pictures of every inept member of staff"

STE: "it's obviously a very delicate time for everyone and –"

JOHN: "It's a joke."

* *

DOUG: I'm alright.

I'm always alright.

Course I am.

> *Beat.*

I'm fine.

I am.

> *Beat.*

But...

> *He thinks. Takes his time.*

No.

* *

STE: You're ten minutes late.

NEIL: What?

DOUG: What time do you call this?

NEIL: You what?

STE: Phone's been going off the hook.

NEIL: Has it?

STE: Yeh it was only Carl though.

NEIL: Shut up!

DOUG: Just checking we were all here ready to start the week.

NEIL: Hey?

STE: Just seeing if we needed anything.

DOUG: "All set?" he said.

NEIL: Nah.

DOUG: "You know what you're up to this week then boys?"

NEIL: Shut up.

JOHN: He did ring.

NEIL: Oh Christ. He didn't?

JOHN: He did.

NEIL: What did you say?

DOUG: What could we say?

STE: Had to tell him the truth.

NEIL: You didn't! You could've said I were on the bog.

DOUG: But you weren't

NEIL: I'm only ten minutes late.

STE: Ten minutes is someone's life Neil.

NEIL: Fucking hell.

STE: I'd start packing that bag.

DOUG: Aye, pack it up son, you'll be on your way later.

NEIL: I can't, I'm not –

JOHN: They're messing with you Neil. He only spoke to me.

NEIL: Really? Thank God. Dicks. What did you say?

JOHN: I said Neil's a lazy fucker he's never here on time.

NEIL: You didn't.

JOHN: Can't get his arse out of bed.

NEIL: John!

* *

STE: "Come in Neil, take a seat."

NEIL: Here?

STE: "There's fine."

NEIL: Thanks.

STE: "How you doing?"

NEIL: Yeh, I'm alright.

STE: "Did Donna get you a tea?"

NEIL: No.

STE: "She didn't?"

NEIL: Didn't want one.

STE: "Right.

>   *Beat.*

> So this is just a quick catch up, just a quick meeting to discuss –"

NEIL: I wasn't late.

STE: "When?"

NEIL: Never.

STE: "Pardon."

NEIL: What?

STE: "This isn't about punctuality."

NEIL: It's not a disciplinary?

STE: "No. It's a one to one."

NEIL: Right.

STE: "Who said it was a disciplinary?"

NEIL: Nothing, no one, they are just having me on.

Beat.

STE: "Are you ok?"

NEIL: Yeh, fine.

STE: "Anything bothering you?"

DOUG: Boots.

STE: "Your boots?"

DOUG: Yeh, they're shit.

STE: "Right."

DOUG: Our last manager – James – he bought DeWalt boots.

STE: "I only –"

DOUG: But these ones are shit.

STE: "I can only order off the portal."

DOUG: Can you order DeWalts off the portal?

STE: "Erm… No."

JOHN: Am I?

STE: "Are you alright?"

JOHN: Yeh… I suppose. Yes.

STE: "Suppose?"

JOHN: Well I mean. I'm fine, you know. It's just…sometimes this job, being what it is, you know. I mean it's a good job, I know that, but sometimes it's –

STE: "Difficult."

JOHN: Yeh.

STE: "Are you finding it difficult at the moment?"

NEIL: The job?

STE: "Yes."

NEIL: I guess so.

STE: "Is there anything I can do to help?"

NEIL: Like what?

STE: "Well what are your issues?"

DOUG: Thermals.

STE: "Thermals?"

DOUG: Yep.

STE: "Why are they an issue?"

DOUG: Because we don't have them. The lads want them but they're too scared to ask.

STE: "You want thermals?"

JOHN: No I'm fine.

NEIL: Thermals? No. What are they?

STE: "They never mentioned them to me."

DOUG: As I said, scared, I sometimes feel like they raise things just so I stick my head up. I don't know why I bother.

STE: "I'll look at costs."

DOUG: It's just...station staff have them and we don't, I'd hate to get the union involved.

STE: "No."

NEIL: No. I don't need anything, I'm alright, it's just a lot of change.

STE: "Yeh. Well honestly I'm always here."

NEIL: Thank you.

STE: "And here's the number for Factor, they offer advice. It's through HR. But it's anonymous."

JOHN: I'm not mental.

STE: "I'm not saying you are."

JOHN: I don't need that.

STE: "That's fine."

NEIL: It's free?

STE: "Yes, you can talk to them about anything, money, work, anything."

NEIL: Thanks.

STE: "What's up?"

JOHN: Huh?

STE: "Your tea? Is something up with it?"

JOHN: Erm –

DOUG: I don't know whether the other lads raised this –

* *

STE: The Jumper.

Just our average job really.

They're the ones who stand there waiting for that announcement which says –

ALL: "Please stand back from the platform edge as the next train does not stop here"

STE: They wait for those because they know they're going faster.

They tend to do it when most trains are running, at or very near stations and they go everywhere.

NEIL: We don't carry water

DOUG: We get it from stations

JOHN: Too heavy

DOUG: And if it's in the middle of nowhere

JOHN: You don't need it

NEIL: Biodegradable

JOHN: Just chuck a bit of sand down

STE: The Winger.

Similar to a jumper only they time it wrong, or get unlucky.

Tend to get winged by the train they're not always dead when you arrive.

NEIL: High vis vest

DOUG: Detachable at the shoulders

NEIL: Hard hat

DOUG: Blue

NEIL: Orange reflective trousers

JOHN: High vis T-Shirt

NEIL: Breathable material

STE: The Platform Crawlers – these are the ones who get clothing caught or fall down the side of the track.

Often lose limbs, occasionally worse, sometimes bounce the length of the platform, smash into tunnel walls, obviously this is a broad category and the injuries and clean-ups vary.

DOUG: Safety boots

JOHN: Steel toe-caps

DOUG: Steel mid-soles

NEIL: Rubber bottoms

JOHN: Ankle supports

DOUG: Shit boots

NEIL: Waterproof

JOHN: Not branded

DOUG: Because the boss is a stingy fucker

STE: The Bouncers.

Almost the exact opposite of the Crawler, and an extension of the Winger.

Imagine you are on a bridge and you jump slightly too late, you hit the train but perhaps the roof, it sends you flying in all directions, spinning out of control, very effective but blood splatter isn't limited to the front end of the train, I once saw a man who hit a Virgin Pendalino, he managed to splatter every carriage.

DOUG: That's it really

NEIL: In terms of –

JOHN: Yeh

NEIL: Erm

JOHN: That's our kit

NEIL: PPE

JOHN: Personal Protective Equipment

NEIL: Sorry

JOHN: And we have the van

DOUG: White

JOHN: Branded

NEIL: Network Rail logo

DOUG: Specialist Cleaning Team

JOHN: "How's my driving?"

DOUG: Shit

STE: Finally… The Popper.

> These people know what they are doing – It's almost as if they've done it before.

> They time it right, perfectly so that they hit the hardest part of the train at its fastest moment.

> The name comes from a water balloon, which acts in much the same way as a human body does when hit by a high speed train.

NEIL: We don't know what we'll see when we arrive

JOHN: Have to be prepared for anything

NEIL: Spillages from freight trains

JOHN: Infrastructure collapses

NEIL: Bridges and that

DOUG: The cows were the worst

NEIL: Aye

DOUG: Two cows hit full speed

JOHN: Looked like a fucking deli counter

STE: You obviously have the idiots as well, who jump in front of a train that changes track right in front of them, end up with two defunct knee joints, some leg bones sticking out and the lingering question of what to do if you can't even kill yourself.

* *

JOHN: I went on holiday. To Croatia. Mrs booked it.

Dubrovnik.

Pricey.

And the thing I remember most about it, the trip.

I mean, don't get me wrong it were hot right, and that was great and the city were pretty impressive. Walled, orange rooves, it were busy. Rammed.

But it was alright.

The thing I remember though was, this Nutella sauce that they served for breakfast. I can't remember the name but it wasn't Nutella. And it was different because you got it in these little plastic tubs right, and half of it was chocolate, milk chocolate, brown. And the other half were white chocolate. Perfect halves. Soft, spreadable like. Not like if you melted chocolate at home and tried to do it.

Anyway, I was blown away by it, we had a continental breakfast everyday with the room, salami, breads, cheeses, pastries and that, but all I ate were this chocolate spread on toast.

I don't even like Nutella.

But I had just never seen it before.

Then, I'm in Tesco and there it is on the shelf, next to Nutella.

There's just no joy anymore is there?

* *

NEIL: Can you stop banging on about it?

DOUG: He said he asked.

JOHN: About thermals?

DOUG: Well about equipment.

JOHN: I don't remember.

STE: He asked me.

DOUG: What did you say?

STE: I said I had some.

DOUG: Fucking hell.

STE: I do.

DOUG: "All for one, one for all!" boys.

NEIL: I said I didn't want them.

DOUG: Oh for the love of God.

JOHN: It was alright weren't it.

STE: Pile of shite.

NEIL: He's not that bad.

STE: Felt like I was talking to myself.

JOHN: Did Donna make you a tea?

DOUG: Aye.

JOHN: How was it?

DOUG: I can't remember.

NEIL: She's alright Donna isn't she?

STE: You think?

JOHN: Mine tasted like piss.

DOUG: Really?

JOHN: Yeh. Literally.

NEIL: I don't mind Carl.

STE: That's because the daft bastard gave you a job.

JOHN: It tasted like piss smells.

STE: What?

JOHN: The tea.

STE: What you on about?

JOHN: Like she'd fished it out with pissy fingers.

NEIL: He gives a shit at least.

DOUG: Gives a shit?

NEIL: I think he does.

DOUG: Gives a shit? Look at your boots Neil, does he give a shit about them?

NEIL: I don't give a shit about them.

STE: Did he mention your punctuality Neil?

NEIL: Piss off.

JOHN: Was it an action?

STE: Improve your timekeeping.

JOHN: Just under 'stop being a penis'.

STE: and man up.

* *

NEIL: MAN UP?

Beat.

Man. Up. Man – Up.

What's that even mean?

It's not even a…it's not even an anything, just two frigging words.

Become a man? Be more male, what do you want from me?

That's what she's saying. She says. She's saying it all the time. Man Up.

How do I do that? What do you mean?

Literally, what do you mean?

Is this how I walk as a man, or stand? Is it? Or do I do it like this? Please fucking tell me what that instruction means!

I am a man. Look at me. I'm male.

Beat.

I feel things. Things hurt me. Does that mean I am not a man, not dealing with things in the way I should as a man?

As a man do I have to be detached? Hard? Do I have to be strong, have arguments, protect my damsel from danger? Do I?

Does that make me a man?

Beat.

I'll hold my hands up. I'm treading water.

I don't know what I am.

I'm treading water without any idea how to swim.

I'm kicking frantically, hoping to stay afloat.

Beat.

I am manning up.

That is what I am doing.

This is me – manning up.

* *

STE: We rock up to this job.

DOUG: And it looks like a quick one.

JOHN: All inside the four.

STE: Foot.

JOHN: What?

Beat.

STE: The four foot.

JOHN: Yeh.

Beat.

NEIL: They don't know what the four is.

JOHN: The four foot?

DOUG: Yeh.

JOHN: It's the tracks.

Look, here's the tracks right.

STE: For the love of God!

JOHN: What? Here's the tracks and this is the four. The middle bit.

STE: What are you doing?

JOHN: Well I don't have a fucking crayon and a flip chart do I?

DOUG: Now if the body lands in this bit then you can get it cleared up in no time.

NEIL: In the four.

STE: But in this case the man had laid himself down on the track.

NEIL: His head sticking over this rail here.

DOUG: The train has come along and whipped his head off.

JOHN: Clean as a whistle.

DOUG: Whoom, just like that.

STE: And his body was lying still, right across the four.

NEIL: But his head.

JOHN: His head was here.

NEIL: No, it were right over here.

STE: Problem is, here, just outside this track, here.

JOHN: Is the live rail.

DOUG: The juice rail.

NEIL: Actually called a "Third Rail".

> *They take a small beat to acknowledge that NEIL knows this information.*

STE: It runs parallel to the others.

JOHN: And it's…

NEIL: Alive with electricity.

DOUG: It's how trains move.

JOHN: The live rail is like a really powerful microwave.

DOUG: It'll cook you from the inside out in seconds.

NEIL: Anyway –

JOHN: Because this guy's head is here.

NEIL: The nice and simple clean up job.

STE: 45 minutes at the most.

DOUG: Becomes a tricky little bugger.

STE: Now we have to do –

JOHN: Risk assessments

NEIL: Isolation requests

DOUG: Line blocks

JOHN: Double checks

DOUG: Triple checks

JOHN: Safety checks

DOUG: In short this is a faff.

NEIL: Ste?

JOHN: Shit.

DOUG: What you doing?

JOHN: He skipped over the rail and legged it down to the head.

DOUG: You can't do that…what are you doing?

NEIL: The rail were still 'live'.

DOUG: And there could be passing trains on the other track.

NEIL: Ste!

STE: I'm sorting us out boys.

JOHN: The station manager was coming.

NEIL: No more than 300 yards away.

DOUG: Two civil policemen pottering along behind her.

NEIL: If they see him.

JOHN: He's fired.

DOUG: That simple.

JOHN: Ste you daft bastard get back over here.

STE: Will do –

JOHN: He said.

STE: But I'm not staying here all night for this.

JOHN: He adjusted his stance.

NEIL: Shuffled his feet.

DOUG: Lined up the head.

NEIL: And toe poked it.

JOHN: It flew

DOUG: High

NEIL: Up

JOHN: Up

DOUG: Up

JOHN: Hair flapping

DOUG: Blood splurting

JOHN: Flying

NEIL: Looping

DOUG: Over the live rail

JOHN: And back into the four

NEIL: Landing nostrils first

DOUG: Bouncing

JOHN: Rolling

DOUG: And stopping by Neil's feet.

NEIL is speechless staring at the head between his feet.

JOHN: Ste skipped back over the rail.

DOUG: And stood there like he'd done nothing wrong.

>   *Beat.*

JOHN: Before we knew it, station manager arrived.

DOUG: "Alright boys, looks like an easy one this."

>   *Beat.*

STE: Yeh.

JOHN: Took his head clean off.

STE: We're lucky it stayed in the four.

DOUG: "Yeh…you alright Neil?"

NEIL: I –

JOHN: You alright for us to start Fran?

DOUG: "Yep, go ahead."

STE: Neil –

NEIL: I… Yeh?

STE: Bag.

DOUG: For the head.

NEIL: Erm… Right… Yeh.

* *

STE: Touch black take it back.

NEIL: Touch white make it right.

DOUG: Sign of the cross.

JOHN: Bow to the bird.

NEIL: The magpie.

JOHN: Magpies.

DOUG: All I see is magpies.

NEIL: Everywhere.

* *

STE: He comes to me every other Friday and stays through until Sunday night.

He sits there and says things like –

NEIL: "What do you prefer Pepsi or Coke?"

STE: And –

NEIL: "When it's my birthday can you get me some skates?"

STE: Or asks questions like –

NEIL: "What is it you do?"

STE: It's getting harder to ignore the ones about work.

NEIL: "Dad? It's for a project.

Beat.

Dad?"

STE: I…err… What does Roger's Dad do?

NEIL: "He's a fireman."

STE: He's a prick.

I make him fish finger sandwiches on Friday nights. White Bread. Butter. Loads of brown sauce.

He likes it I think.

It's for a project?

NEIL: "Yeh."

STE: Right.

On Saturdays we sometimes pop to the local and I treat him. Hunters chicken or beef pie, and chips, again – obviously.

Well… I help make sure the trains are running on time.

NEIL: "Is that it?"

STE: No… I…erm…clean the tracks when they get mucky.

We should never really have got married. His mum and me. I was 19 and she was 18, we just thought – that was what you did, you get married.

You get married and you have kids, you get a house and that's what you do.

NEIL: "Mucky?"

STE: Mucky…dirty. With mud and stuff.

NEIL: "You clean mud off tracks, is that a job?"

STE: No I…what? No, it's not just mud.

Beat.

Well – sometimes people jump in front of trains.

NEIL: "Awesome!"

STE: No not really.

NEIL: "Why do they do that?"

STE: Because they're not very happy.

Beat.

NEIL: "Do you see brains and guts and stuff?"

STE: Not answering that.

I used to maintain the train carriage cleaners in the depots, and from there it just made sense to do this. More money.

NEIL: "Do you take pictures?"

STE: No.

NEIL: "I bet you have to take pictures"

STE: She left me when I was 23. We had nothing in common, nothing, apart from the baby, it wasn't nasty, it still isn't, I loved her…once, but it was when I was working out what that meant. I loved her but in the way that you like looking at rivers until you see the sea.

* *

JOHN: Fucking hell Neil.

NEIL: What?

JOHN: Where's the bloody light?

NEIL: What?

JOHN: The light you tit.

NEIL: Oh sorry.

NEIL turns on his torch.

JOHN: I told you my battery was on the blink.

NEIL: Yeh.

JOHN: Right, hold still.

Beat.

NEIL: I don't like this.

JOHN: What?

NEIL: Being out here in the dark.

JOHN: You're afraid of the dark?

NEIL: No.

Beat.

What was that?

JOHN: Oh for God's sake.

NEIL: What was it?

JOHN: You? Me?

NEIL: Nah, it wasn't. Sounded big?

JOHN: Just look over here or we'll be here all bloody night.

Beat.

Neil?

NEIL: Sorry.

Beat.

How was the holiday?

JOHN: Alright.

NEIL: Good. Where was it you /

JOHN: Croatia.

NEIL: That's it.

> *Beat.*

Where's that then?

JOHN: Europe.

NEIL: Right. Nice?

JOHN: Hot.

NEIL: Nice.

What was that?

JOHN: Oh, for fuck's sake.

> *NEIL's light goes off and STE and DOUG illuminate theirs.*

DOUG: How's the lad?

STE: Yeh, he's good. Getting bigger.

DOUG: Yeh, they do that.

> *Beat.*

He's alright though?

STE: Yeh.

> *Beat.*

DOUG: How old is he now?

STE: Coming up on ten.

DOUG: Shit.

STE: Yeh.

> *Beat.*

You going to have kids?

DOUG: Nah.

STE: Really?

DOUG: No.

Beat.

STE: Mrs doesn't fancy any?

DOUG: Nah.

> *DOUG turns his light off, STE waits a moment then turns off his own.*

JOHN: Jesus, Neil!

NEIL: What?

JOHN: What do you mean what? We're in the bloody dark again.

NEIL: I know.

JOHN: So turn on the light.

Beat.

NEIL: I can't.

JOHN: Why?

NEIL: I think the batteries have gone.

* *

STE: "I was on-track cleaning and maintenance manager for Network Rail at the…erm…at the time. I'm Carl, Carl Bates."

JOHN: "Deborah McKay, psychiatrist, I deal with post-incident care for train drivers, passengers and railway staff."

STE: "I managed most of the on-track maintenance. Anything from vegetation to…well, obviously…obstruction clearance."

JOHN: "Sometimes my role is over in a matter of hours, most of the time it can be part of an ongoing support package."

STE: "I remember the day very well."

JOHN: "Yes. I was involved with this particular case.

I would like to keep this fairly vague if that's ok?

I provided sessions for the driver, and several members of Network Rail staff who were closely involved with the individual."

STE: "It was a horrible day. The worst.

I knew the guy. I knew him. Do you know what I mean?"

JOHN: "There were no witnesses with that one, which was a positive.

They can be the tricky ones. Children particularly so."

STE: "I had met with them the previous week, all of them, one to one, I asked them... I asked him."

JOHN: "I have also dealt with those who are contemplating suicide."

STE: "Is there anything I should know?"

ALL: No.

STE: "Anything I can do for you?"

ALL: No.

STE: "He said no."

JOHN: "There are trends on the railway, patterns. They tend to be lost, looking for an outlet. It's often a spontaneous act. Not a series of deteriorating symptoms. It's generally men. From poorer socio-economic groups, with a history of mental health problems. They often leave little behind."

STE: "I felt like I –"

JOHN: "No notes, no letters to loved ones. They are incapable of focusing on the impact, on the legacy of their choice. Their focus is entirely on the moment not the ramifications."

STE: "Obviously I felt... I could have done more."

JOHN: "Reasonable people, who for that moment become impervious to reason. Detached from sentiment."

STE: "I did. I still do."

* *

DOUG: A report in 2015 claimed that 305 people a year took their own life on the railways.

JOHN: Doesn't sound much does it?

NEIL: But when you think there were just over 6,500 suicides in total.

JOHN: It puts it in perspective.

NEIL: Nearly 5%.

DOUG: All the bridges you can jump off.

STE: The pills you can swallow.

NEIL: The branches you can hang from.

STE: And 5% end their life this way.

JOHN: Almost one a day.

STE: Every 31 hours.

JOHN: Most male.

NEIL: Most between the age of 30 and 55.

DOUG: Our age.

STE: Most from poorer families.

NEIL: Poorer areas.

DOUG: Most poor.

NEIL: In 2010, there were 218 suicides on the railway.

JOHN: Every 38.4 hours.

STE: Suicide delays cost the government –

NEIL: £33 million a year.

JOHN: Compensation to the TOC.

NEIL: Train operating company.

JOHN: Yep – sorry.

DOUG: Line blocks.

JOHN: Clean-up teams.

STE: Support teams.

DOUG: Both emotional and physical.

JOHN: Isolations.

STE: The list goes on.

JOHN: The problem is now so bad.

DOUG: That they employ teams to deal with it.

JOHN: Us in the North.

NEIL: And another down South.

* *

STE: Arrive

JOHN: Clock starts

STE: Engine off

NEIL: Greet

JOHN: Meet

DOUG: Talk

NEIL: Pass – bag

STE: And –

JOHN: Off, we're off

STE: Ten minutes on the clock

NEIL: Here

STE: Pass – bag

JOHN: Over here

NEIL: Pass – bag

DOUG: Here

NEIL: Pass – bag

DOUG: And here

STE: Pass – bag

NEIL: Sand

JOHN: Lots of sand

STE: Pouring sand

DOUG: And one

NEIL: and another

STE: And here

JOHN: Over there

DOUG: And here

NEIL: Pass – bag

STE: and here

DOUG: Pass – bag

STE: Skin

JOHN: Bones

DOUG: Pass – bag

STE: Blood

JOHN: Bits

NEIL: Pass – bag

DOUG: Over here

NEIL: Clothes

STE: Rings

JOHN: Pass – bag

NEIL: Here

STE: Pass – bag

NEIL: And here

DOUG: Pass – bag

JOHN: Faster

STE: Spray

DOUG: And spray

STE: Power spray

JOHN: Wash away

NEIL: Here

DOUG: Wash, wash

NEIL: And here

STE: Wash, wash

JOHN: Then

NEIL: Tidy up

JOHN: Hurry up

STE: Cleaning up

JOHN: Quickly

DOUG: Flag it

NEIL: Bag it

JOHN: Tag it

STE: Bleach it

JOHN: Spray it

DOUG: Done

NEIL: Pass – bag

JOHN: Yep

DOUG: Done

NEIL: Pass – bag

JOHN: We're done

DOUG: Ignition

JOHN: Stop the clock.

Beat.

STE: 80 minutes.

They are disappointed.

* *

NEIL: It wasn't like they said, I'll go that far.

Sorry. Is anyone pregnant here?

I don't want to be that dick that goes too far while you're sitting there thinking it'll be like a Disney film. Thinking you'll be singing songs while sparrows wrap a ribbon around the baby's head.

45

JOHN: This is –

DOUG: "Stanley."

JOHN: Hi Stanley, how old are you Stanley?

DOUG: "I'm six."

JOHN: He's six.

NEIL: Sixteen hours of screaming. Before we went to the hospital. Sixteen hours of bouncing on a ball. Leaning on walls. On me. Meditating. Crying.

I hadn't helped, I'd done nothing, felt useless, just flicking buttons on a TENS machine, adjusting pads, offering water, breathe I was saying, breathe. All I could think of, as if she'd forget. I was useless.

DOUG: "I was with my dad."

STE: "Hi."

JOHN: His dad is called –

STE: "Tom."

JOHN: Hi Tom.

STE: "Alright."

NEIL: At the hospital – gas and air, wasn't enough, she needed something stronger, tears, screaming, I was dabbing her head, trying to be something, to do something to make it easier, I wasn't, I couldn't. An epidural helped, but the baby got stuck, it was back to back and its heart rate rocketed, I remember words like 'distressed' and 'operate' and before I knew it we were in theatre. She was scared. She was looking at me to help, to fix it. I couldn't.

JOHN: What were you doing Stan?

DOUG: "We were waiting for the train."

JOHN: Just waiting?

DOUG: "Waiting and playing."

NEIL: When the baby came, a girl, a little girl, she 'needed assistance' someone had said, her airways were blocked.

She went straight onto a gurney and down a corridor. Everything was 'routine', that's what people were saying, 'it's routine', but nothing felt routine. I went with the baby, to the special care unit. The first time I wrote her name I was signing a disclaimer. Emily.

JOHN: Why were you playing?

DOUG: "It was fun."

JOHN: It's not a playground though is it Stan?

DOUG: "No."

JOHN: It's very dangerous son.

DOUG: "I know."

NEIL: 'I never got to hold her,' Nic said. 'They took her before I held her.' I couldn't say anything, I couldn't comfort her. She'd cry when she said it. The baby was back with us, she was fine, but it was like she wasn't.

I hugged her, Nic, held her, but I couldn't – they had to stay in, both of them, I had to go home every night, to leave her, to leave the baby. Emily. In the mornings when I got back it was like everything had got worse. The nurses noticed, I think but –

She was agitated. Scared.

That was my first weeks paternity leave.

JOHN: And what were you doing?

STE: "Hey?"

JOHN: While he was playing?

STE: "I was… I was."

JOHN: What?

STE: "I was on my phone."

JOHN: On your phone?

STE: "…Yeh."

NEIL: I asked Carl to extend my leave, told him what had happened. Said I needed more time, I needed to be here.

He wouldn't, couldn't, our leave is done on rotas, 'It's hard,' he said, 'I'm so sorry,' I asked if I could take emergency leave and he said I could take five days, 'best he could do'.

JOHN: Making a call?

STE: "No."

JOHN: Emails?

STE: "No."

JOHN: What then?

STE: "I was – Facebook."

JOHN: Right.

STE: "I didn't think –"

NEIL: Nicola couldn't move because of the operation, when I was home I was doing everything. Bed time, midnight feed, 2 AM, 4 AM, 6. I was trying to make it better, to make it easier. But with work –

JOHN: You weren't doing enough were you?

STE: "No"

JOHN: Not nearly enough.

STE: "No."

NEIL: I was tired – shattered. We both were. Emily was on formula all the time because Nic refused to have her near her when she was crying…problem was every time I took her near her she'd cry, and that made it worse, it made it harder, for both of them.

I looked at them – both, I was failing them.

DOUG: "I was just playing and I tripped."

STE: "He tripped over."

JOHN: Right.

STE: "And the train it was already coming."

JOHN: It's alright.

NEIL: It's hard, I want to be here, I want be there, I don't know where I am, where I should be, I don't know anything, nothing, I'm lost. I want to help. I want to help them, both of them, but I don't know how. It's like I'm playing a game without the rule book. A game that should be fun – but it's shit.

I tell you, what I would've given for a sparrow and a fucking ribbon.

STE: "I tried to –"

JOHN: Yeh.

STE: "It was too late."

JOHN: I bet you wish you could'/ve…

STE: "I do."

JOHN: I bet it's hard.

> *STE nods. Sits. Defeated.*

> *A long pause.*

* *

STE: It was this kid. About six.

Tiny.

He was messing around, near the platform edge, he was hit hard.

He had no chance.

His dad, was sat down with the police when we arrived.

His face red, puffy, tears streaming from his eyes.

He couldn't –

> *Beat.*

He couldn't breathe. Couldn't focus on anything.

He was holding his kid's bag still, this little blue, red and yellow bag.

This tiny little thing.

As we arrived they took him inside, he couldn't move.

He wanted to stay where he was, he was screaming, but no words you could recognise, just these horrible growls, these gut-wrenching screams.

We walked past him with sponges and buckets of water and he was dragged the other way with that little bag.

That was…that's when you –

> *Beat.*

That…in my heart, I felt that. In my heart. As if I was that man. As if I was clinging onto that little bag.

That's when the worry started, the doubts, worries, that's when they started.

* *

NEIL: What've you got there?

> *Beat. JOHN notices.*

JOHN: Hey?

NEIL: What you eating?

JOHN: Sushi.

DOUG: Course you are.

NEIL: What's that?

JOHN: Sushi?

NEIL: Yeh.

JOHN: It's –

DOUG: It's too posh for you mate!

JOHN: Like rice wrapped with fish in it.

NEIL: You what?

JOHN: It's fish and rice.

NEIL: Cold?

JOHN: Yeh.

NEIL: You what?

STE: He's never seen anything like this John.

DOUG: Blowing his mind look at him.

JOHN: It's been around a while.

NEIL: You're eating it cold?

JOHN: Yeh, its raw.

NEIL: Raw?

JOHN: Yeh. It's fish.

NEIL: What's that it's wrapped in?

JOHN: Seaweed.

NEIL: Sorry?

STE: Seaweed.

NEIL: Has someone got a camera on me?

STE: What?

NEIL: Is this a wind up? That's seaweed and that's raw fish?

JOHN: Yeh.

NEIL: Why are you eating this shit John?

DOUG: It's healthy.

NEIL: It don't bloody look healthy. What's that?

JOHN: Soya sauce.

NEIL: Right.

DOUG: What, you've heard of that?

NEIL: Yeh. What's that?

JOHN: You'll like that try a bit.

NEIL: What is it?

JOHN: Try it.

NEIL: Is it fish?

JOHN: No, try it.

He does.

NEIL: Fucking hell.

DOUG: That's wasabi you daft bastard!

NEIL: Fucking – me tongue.

* *

DOUG: Am I Johnny big bollocks? Leader of the pack?

Beat.

No.

Not really.

Beat.

It's who I've become.

It's a habit.

I sometimes hear myself say things and a second after I wish I could take it back.

Sometimes I wish I could take it back before I've even said it. Like I know that I am about to say something I don't mean. Then I say it anyway.

I'm not a dick.

But I know that I am.

That I've become one.

Beat.

It's not – I'm not angry – I'm –

* *

JOHN: It was back there.

STE: It weren't.

JOHN: I'm telling you it was back there.

NEIL: You can get this way.

STE: You don't just "get" this way, this is the way.

JOHN: I promise you it was back there, with the big bloody station sign.

DOUG: I think there's road works.

JOHN: Thank you.

DOUG: Just beyond the lights there, can you see.

STE: Is there?

JOHN: Is there…now he's bloody interested.

STE: Shit.

NEIL: Can you not get past 'em?

DOUG: Well you can get past them but I'm not sure you'd want to.

JOHN: For God's sake.

STE: Shhhhh I'm trying to think.

JOHN: Think?

STE: Shh.

JOHN: U-turn, how hard's that? Turn around, go back to the lights and listen to me.

STE: Shut up.

NEIL: There, there's a diversion sign.

DOUG: Diversion, the bloody station is there, I can see it. How far we going to go on a diversion?

STE: Shhh.

NEIL: Well what's the point in the diversion sign?

DOUG: It's for people going a bit bloody further than 400 yards.

JOHN: We've been here before haven't we.

DOUG: Yep.

NEIL: Were it recent?

DOUG: Nah, about a year.

NEIL: Bad one?

DOUG: I can't remember.

STE: I think it were a girl.

DOUG: That's it.

JOHN: Weren't you driving then too?

STE: Think so.

JOHN: Bloody idiot.

STE: Young girl?

DOUG: Yeh, it was, I remember that.

* *

DOUG: This is

JOHN: Peter

NEIL: Peter's a dick head

JOHN: "Hey –"

STE: You are

DOUG: Yeh

NEIL: Everyone thinks it

DOUG: He has spent his life being a bit of a cock

STE: But Peter is about to become a legendary dick head

JOHN: "Am I?"

NEIL: Yes

DOUG: Peter is a solicitor

STE: Quite a successful one

JOHN: "Thank you"

STE: He handles minor family law cases

DOUG: And, he has no previous diagnosed mental health conditions

NEIL: Yay

STE: Clean bill of health

NEIL: He is raking in a whopping

JOHN: "Circa £72,000"

NEIL: Plus

JOHN: "Bonuses"

DOUG: Wow

STE: Good man

NEIL: Married

DOUG: Two kids

STE: Two cars

NEIL: Peter eats well

STE: Votes Tory

NEIL: Reads the Daily Telegraph

STE: Is blind to the problems of others

DOUG: He works hard

NEIL: And holidays harder

STE: Dick head

JOHN: "No, I give to charity"

NEIL: He does

STE: Yeh

DOUG: Not much

JOHN: "No – but –"

DOUG: A little

JOHN: "I give what I can"

STE: Yeh

DOUG: Hold the phone

NEIL: Put the brakes on

STE: Woah there

JOHN: "What?"

STE: I think Peter's holding something back

DOUG: What's this?

STE: Something is coming over the horizon

DOUG: Just popping its little head up to say hello

JOHN: "There isn't"

DOUG: Oh I think there is Pete

NEIL: I think there bloody might be my mate

STE: Peter has been stealing from clients

DOUG: Oh no

JOHN: "I haven't"

NEIL: That was his defence

DOUG: But the police didn't buy it

JOHN: "I wouldn't"

STE: His wife didn't buy it either

NEIL: But, where did the money go?

STE: On the house?

NEIL: The cars?

DOUG: The kids?

STE: No

NEIL: No, no, no, no, no

STE: Pete has spent the money on filthy nights with dirty girls

JOHN: "I would never"

DOUG: There are witnesses

STE: And bank statements

NEIL: Understandably these charges

JOHN: "Accusations"

NEIL: No, charges

STE: Are all getting a bit much for our loveable rogue

DOUG: And one day

NEIL: In the early morning

STE: He rolls out of bed

DOUG: Drives to the station

NEIL: Parks the car

STE: Pays for a three day parking ticket

DOUG: Sticks it on the underside of his windscreen

STE: Walks to his boot

DOUG: Takes his jacket and briefcase from where they lay

NEIL: Walks past the other cars

DOUG: Down the steps to the platform

STE: He hears the announcement

NEIL: He waits

STE: He hears the announcement again

NEIL: He takes a deep breath

DOUG: He hears a train

STE: A screeching

NEIL: Creaking train

STE: The hum of the rails

DOUG: The scratching of wheels

NEIL: He takes another breath

DOUG: His heart is racing

STE: His mind racing

DOUG: His head's aching

NEIL: Another breath

STE: Deeper

DOUG: Longer

STE: Screeching

DOUG: Wailing

NEIL: Another

JOHN: "Breath"

NEIL: Another

JOHN: "Breath"

NEIL: Another

STE: And he just does it –

>   *Beat.*

JOHN: "How does that make me a dick?"

STE: Because Pete

DOUG: It's rush hour

NEIL: And you jumped in front of a high speed train

STE: At a very busy station

DOUG: And –

STE: There's a party of school children heading into town

NEIL: Going to a museum

DOUG: Only they don't make it

NEIL: Because you are all over them

STE: Literally

DOUG: Like a wave of gunge

JOHN: "Right"

STE: That's a bit thoughtless isn't it Pete

JOHN: "I didn't notice – I didn't see – I wasn't thinking of –"

NEIL: Them

JOHN: "No"

DOUG: Dick head.

* *

Silence. They are back in the van.

NEIL: That was –

JOHN: Yeh.

NEIL: Yeh.

Beat.

STE: Horrible.

DOUG: Messy.

Pause.

JOHN: I was right though.

STE: What?

JOHN: It was that first left back there.

* *

NEIL: I cross the magpie.

STE: The magpie crosses me.

DOUG: Bad luck to the magpie.

JOHN: And good luck to me.

NEIL: One for sorrow.

STE: Two for joy.

DOUG: Three for a girl.

JOHN: Four for a boy.

* *

NEIL: We do other cleaning to 'keep us busy'

STE: Planned not reactive

JOHN: High level windows

STE: Jet washing platforms

DOUG: Removing chewing gum from forecourts

JOHN: Deep clean of toilets

DOUG: And we clean light fittings

STE: Which is shit

DOUG: It's all shit

NEIL: It is

JOHN: But it's a job

NEIL: Yeh

JOHN: A good job with –

NEIL: Pressure

DOUG: Washer

NEIL: Here

JOHN: There's always pressure

DOUG: That's not new

STE: But money's tighter

NEIL: Time shorter

DOUG: Prices higher

NEIL: So we have additional

DOUG: Pressure

STE: Washer

DOUG: Here

JOHN: Here

NEIL: I can't… It's hard to describe

STE: Some days, most days, it's nothing, it is not anything, but others –

NEIL: It's like pressure

JOHN: Washer

DOUG: Here

STE: Here

DOUG: Sometimes it's starting that's the difficult bit.

Picking where to wipe, what to collect. How to start.

That's sometimes the hardest bit.

NEIL: A silence, before we begin, I always like to just have a small moment.

Just a moment, a second.

DOUG: You look at it, the body, the remains, the job and for a moment you feel like it's wrong to disturb the scene, like it's a shrine.

STE: Here

JOHN: Here

NEIL: I think of it as a minutes silence but it's more like ten seconds.

Just to think of what they've done, what we're doing.

Just a moment to acknowledge that this is weird.

DOUG: After you start you forget it is someone, it is literally someone.

Someone's son. Dad. Someone's sister.

You forget it when you start.

NEIL: It's weird.

DOUG: So sometimes it's literally picking up the cloth, or putting on the gloves that's the hardest bit. Because that's when it's a person.

NEIL: I like to acknowledge that.

DOUG: After that, it's just a mess. Just a job.

STE: Over here.

* *

JOHN: If you make it to 82. That gives you 30,000 days – to live.

30,000.

The first 6,000 are lost to youth.

The last 2 to senility.

That gives you 22,000 days to define who you are.

To be what you are.

It's hard that isn't it.

It's hard to imagine, hard to hear.

If you imagine piles of pound coins.

Thirty thousand of them.

Built over a lifetime, pound by pound. Each one the same in many respects, but with different dents, bruises. Different memories.

They're piled one by one. Coin by coin.

One then another. Until the stack reaches 365 and then a new pile is started. 82 piles.

Every morning I wake up.

I sit in my bed. Throat dry. Eyes sore.

I sit there and I think about throwing another fucking coin on that pile.

Another day older, another pound poorer.

* *

DOUG: There are patterns

STE: The Loner –

NEIL: Tell-tale signs

JOHN: Specific to the railway

STE: Who stands at the end of the platform deep in thought

DOUG: He isn't talking to anyone

JOHN: Just standing

STE: Coat pulled tight around him

NEIL: He stares

DOUG: At nothing specific

NEIL: Just stares ahead

STE: Lost in his own thoughts

JOHN: The Bridge Dweller

DOUG: Standing with both hands on the hand rail

NEIL: Looking out to the horizon

JOHN: Arms locked

DOUG: Tense

STE: There's a lot going on

JOHN: His eyes may shut from time to time

DOUG: The movie of his life projecting on his closed lids

NEIL: He is calm

STE: No aggression

DOUG: Relieved

JOHN: There is a chance

STE: A window of opportunity

DOUG: To rescue them

STE: Not always

DOUG: But sometimes

STE: Sometimes

NEIL: There is

JOHN: It's called intervention

STE: It works

JOHN: "Hello?"

DOUG: Just making contact

JOHN: "Hello, mate, are you alright?"

NEIL: Just noticing them

JOHN: "Are you sure?"

STE: Reminding them that someone is there

DOUG: Giving them a hope

NEIL: A reason

JOHN: "I just… I just wanted to check."

STE: To intervene

NEIL: To interrupt

JOHN: For every suicide there are believed to be three interventions

DOUG: Three

STE: Three more people

NEIL: Three lives saved

JOHN: Every 8 hours someone seriously contemplates jumping in front of a train.

* *

NEIL: I don't know how to sort this.

For her.

I don't –

I don't have answers.

I thought I would have them, by now, the answers.

I don't.

* *

STE: This is

JOHN: "Beryl."

STE: And this is

DOUG: "Colin."

NEIL: They're married

STE: Have been for 52 years

JOHN: "Love you."

DOUG: "I know you do."

NEIL: Beryl joined the RAF during WW2

JOHN: "Travelled the world."

STE: Belgium, Paris and finally

JOHN: "Dorset."

NEIL: He was based there for a short while.

DOUG: "We were just in a pub."

NEIL: When they met

STE: Just minding their own business

NEIL: She noticed him

STE: He noticed her

JOHN: "What's your name?"

STE: She asked

DOUG: "Colin."

NEIL: He replied

JOHN: "I'm Beryl."

STE: He took her address and called on her when the war had ended

NEIL: She was happy with that

JOHN: "Very romantic."

NEIL: They wed

JOHN: "Love you."

DOUG: "I know you do."

NEIL: They had kids and lived their lives

STE: Beryl worked at

JOHN: "The local store, then at the school"

STE: And then finally

JOHN: "At Tesco."

NEIL: And Colin worked

DOUG: "In haulage."

NEIL: Low paid

JOHN: "But happy."

STE: After they retired because

JOHN: "I was 62."

NEIL: And

DOUG: "My eyesight weren't…"

JOHN: "It wasn't what it used to be was it?"

DOUG: "It wasn't."

JOHN: "No."

STE: They expected to live in the relative comfort that they had earned

NEIL: But…

STE: They didn't own their house

JOHN: "No."

STE: And they hadn't really got any savings

NEIL: They'd spent it on

JOHN: "The grandkids."

STE: And

DOUG: "Cruises."

NEIL: Their pension wasn't what they thought

JOHN: "We took a big lump sum."

DOUG: "But we didn't –"

JOHN: "Just didn't calculate it."

DOUG: "Didn't get the sums right."

NEIL: So when the eviction letter came, they were somewhat at a loss

STE: They'd lived in the flat for 15 years

DOUG: "And just down the road before that."

STE: Colin's health was

JOHN: "Deteriorating."

DOUG: "It was."

JOHN: "You're not as strong as you used to be are you?"

DOUG: "No."

NEIL: And Beryl hadn't dealt with money for thirty years

JOHN: "Colin is the numbers man."

DOUG: "Yep."

STE: And also

NEIL: She couldn't bear the thought

JOHN: "I couldn't live without him."

DOUG: "She's my left arm."

JOHN: "And he's my right."

STE: One evening, they ate their tea

JOHN: "Just sausage and mash."

NEIL: Watched *Coronation Street*

STE: Hoovered the front room

NEIL: Puffed up the pillows

STE: Took a look at the photographs lining the hallway

JOHN: "One by one."

DOUG: "Face by face."

STE: Then they put on their coats

NEIL: Pulled on their wellies

STE: Carefully locked the front door

NEIL: And walked through the field at the back of the street

STE: They negotiated the small wooden fence

DOUG: "Careful now."

NEIL: They wandered down to the track and stood

JOHN: "Love you."

STE: She said squeezing his hand

DOUG: "I know you do."

NEIL: He answered as the light began to creep up his face

DOUG: "I love you too."

* *

STE: "Hello team."

> *Beat.*

NEIL: Alright Carl?

STE: "How are we all?"

JOHN: Alright.

DOUG: Alright?

STE: "Are you not alright Doug?"

DOUG: Let's see why we're here first.

STE: "Fine, lets make a start.

> Got a bit of news for you. Nothing that will have a direct effect on you, but in a few months I will be taking up a new role in the department. A little bit of a promotion.

> *Beat.*

> Nothing changes for the moment but we'll be advertising to fill my position soon."

DOUG: Are you changing the structure of the department?

STE: "Erm… No."

DOUG: Is that official? There are going to be no changes to the department.

STE: "Well, we work in a flexible area Doug, so there will always be some degree of change to fit the demand"

DOUG: But, to our positions, there won't be any changes.

STE: "Has someone been filling you head with things Doug?"

> *Beat.*

DOUG: Sorry?

STE: "I mean –"

DOUG: Has someone been filling my head?

STE: "Well –"

DOUG: Are you suggesting that my head is incapable of filling itself?

STE: "Of course not."

DOUG: Because Carl, though you have been on the railway 5 minutes lad, I've worked in some area or another all my adult life, so you come in here with your fancy packs of paper and your neatly ironed shirt and you expect us to respect you, and we do, we go along with your performance reviews and your one to ones, because if that's how you like to waste your time, then we'll help you. But on the railway lad, people talk, so no, no one has been filling my head with anything, they have been passing on snippets of information gathered from meetings you've had.

So can I ask you again, and this time let me assure you I expect a satisfactory response. Can you confirm that there will be no alterations to our jobs? Yes or no?

STE: "There will currently be no changes to your positions."

DOUG: Was that a yes or a no?

STE: "That was a response to your question.

> *Beat.*

Alright… Anybody have any questions on structural changes or on…the news that… I…you know?

> *Beat.*

No.

Right. Moving on… Performance… Here is a line graph that indicates how many jobs you have done so far this annum compared to the previous years."

* *

DOUG: FUCK OFF!

It's the pressure, the pressure.

To be strong. To be right!

It's a pressure.

It hurts. Here. All the time.

I take tablets but then I realise it isn't actual.

It isn't a real pain, it's more than that. It's like my brain is screaming.

It's screaming for me to calm down, for me to take it easy. To wind down.

It is screaming at me relax. Fucking relax!

> *Beat.*

But I can't.

I can't.

> *Beat.*

I don't think I can.

* *

NEIL: I'm in the belly of the beast

JOHN: The eye of the storm

STE: My head is –

DOUG: Frazzled

STE: Spinning

NEIL: Dehydrated

STE: Swirling

JOHN: A whirlwind

STE: I'm spinning

DOUG: Noise

NEIL: Noises

JOHN: In my head

DOUG: There's a build up of noise and I want to

NEIL: Scream

DOUG: Shout

JOHN: Cry

STE: I'm Spinning

JOHN: Vision

STE: Spinning

JOHN: People blurring

NEIL: Reflections

STE: Shadows

NEIL: Ghosts

STE: Blurs

NEIL: Breath

STE: Panting

DOUG: Questions

STE: Laughing

JOHN: Normal

NEIL: But at the same time

STE: Shrinking

JOHN: Like a crisp packet in a fire

NEIL: Wrinkling

DOUG: Crinkling

NEIL: Shrinking away

JOHN: Hiding in plain sight

STE: Lost

DOUG: But aware

STE: Lost

NEIL: Screaming

DOUG: But aware

STE: Both a figment

NEIL: Shouting

STE: A figment and an imagination at the same time

DOUG: Bills

NEIL: Nappies

JOHN: Conversations

STE: Bills

JOHN: About holidays

NEIL: Nappies

JOHN: Shit TV

NEIL: Endless nappies and tears

STE: Shouting

NEIL: Screaming

JOHN: Round and round

NEIL: I'm on a carousel

JOHN: Earn money

DOUG: Spend money

STE: No money

NEIL: Need sleep, don't sleep, want sleep – round and round

JOHN: A carousel

STE: With no exit, and no brakes

DOUG: That –

JOHN: is how –

NEIL: I feel

JOHN: Sometimes

DOUG: That is how

JOHN: That's how it feels.

* *

DOUG: "Morning #CommuterTweeps! How are we this Tuesday?

My name is Elaine Chambers. I work in the Social Media section of the Comms department."

NEIL: "Trains late again. #typical."

DOUG: "@snugglebug827 I'm so sorry to hear that your train is delayed, there are signalling problems around Warrington, we're hoping this is all cleared up by 9AM."

STE: "#Lovely member of staff at Liverpool Lime Street helped my Mum on to the train thanks again."

DOUG: "Retweet. Retweet. Retweet."

JOHN: "I hate trains, I hate trains, I hate trains. #joke #delays #hatetrains."

DOUG: "Nothing I can do with that really."

JOHN: "Some prick has jumped in front of my train and now I am late for interview. Absolute farce #selfish."

DOUG: "@RichardGunn25 Sorry about the interview – Always refer back to their original message makes it look like
you tailor specific responses to all customer concerns – we have an ongoing situation in your area – Don't mention specific areas this can lead to copycat suicides – we have a team on site who hope to have you moving soon. Nothing provocative, nothing procedural, simple. 140 characters. Apology, fact, fact, fact."

* *

NEIL: This is

STE: "Mike."

NEIL: He is –

DOUG: Erm –

JOHN: Mike is…male

NEIL: Looks about 50 but he's probably in his mid thirties

DOUG: We'll be honest

JOHN: No one really knows a lot about Mike

NEIL: He's –

STE: "Homeless."

DOUG: Lives off

STE: "Food bank donations."

DOUG: And

STE: "Anything I can make from strangers."

NEIL: He plays the guitar

DOUG: But he's a bit shit

JOHN: In another life he was in the army

STE: "Two tours of Iraq."

DOUG: Not any more

STE: "No. Discharged."

JOHN: With undiagnosed mental health conditions

STE: "Yep."

NEIL: Yep

JOHN: Mike was a popper.

* *

NEIL: Friends.

JOHN: Yes.

NEIL: Yeh.

STE: Erm –

DOUG: I do. Of course I do.

NEIL: Lots, on Facebook and that. People I'm in touch with yeh.

DOUG: I have a few, I'd trust, you know to support me.

JOHN: We have 'couple friends'.

DOUG: Just a few.

STE: No.

DOUG: I mean, I don't need support, you know, but if I want it.

STE: Not really. Work mates. I guess.

NEIL: Yeh.

JOHN: My friends are her friends, collective friends.

DOUG: Family is in Newcastle. So –

JOHN: Dinner date friends – not pint and a clear the air chat friends.

NEIL: I have a few from home, from school you know. My family is nearby but –

DOUG: I don't tend to need to – talk, you know.

STE: Yeh, mates from work. Is that strange? I don't feel like that's strange.

DOUG: I'm not a big talker.

STE: Where do you meet friends now?

There's no dating app that I know that's just for finding someone to have a pint with. Is there? I don't really know the neighbours.

I like the pub, the local, but how often you going to sit drinking on your own?

DOUG: So… Yeh.

NEIL: They're nearby but we're not that close, if you get me.

JOHN: And if they were, I still wouldn't speak to them.

STE: Do you know what I mean?

JOHN: I probably wouldn't.

DOUG: I'd talk to the Mrs.

NEIL: I don't know who I'd –

STE: I just keep my own counsel, I leave work, reluctantly and I go home. That's what I do. Work, home.

And if I've had a bad day, or a bad feeling about someone, something, if I'm bothered by something then I think it over, and normally, by the time I get home it's gone, it's no longer a problem.

JOHN: Luckily I'm no head case, but if I were –

NEIL: I don't know.

JOHN: God, it's hard that, because it'd get back to her.

DOUG: Yeh, I'd talk to her. I think.

JOHN: Don't know. Genuinely.

STE: I walk because it clears my head, frees me up. Rain makes you think clearer. So doesn't matter the weather, I walk home, thinking. That's my thinking time.

JOHN: Sad that innit?

* *

NEIL: Are we done?

STE: It's not three yet.

NEIL: I know but, do you reckon we can get off?

STE: No I don't.

> *Beat.*

NEIL: I'm going to go.

JOHN: You've only just got here Neil.

DOUG: Yeh, you've only just turned up and now you want to leave?

NEIL: Piss off.

JOHN: Lets give it until ten to.

NEIL: I don't see the point.

STE: What of working your contracted hours?

NEIL: No. Of sitting in the bloody van doing nothing.

STE: Because we're paid to?

JOHN: Because it's our job?

NEIL: What time is it now?

DOUG: Half past.

NEIL: Are you joking?

DOUG: How is that a joke?

* *

STE: I don't go around all day thinking about him, but it's nice to think he's doing something, that wherever he is, he's moving, talking, breathing, that he is there.

That's nice.

> *Beat. He pulls out his wallet and removes a photograph he offers it as evidence to the audience.*

He looks like his mum, they're her eyes.

> *Beat. He slowly puts the picture away again.*

He disappears though. For me. He can disappear.

It's easy to forget. To forget his face. His voice.

I start questioning whether I remember him or if I'm remembering photographs of him.

Whether it's memories or pictures.

And then I feel like I have lost him.

That he has gone.

And I start to – I need to speak to him, see him, even a new picture or video on the phone, just to know he is still there. Just to ground me, to give me a fix, he's my drug.

I'm an addict.

> *Beat.*

I need to see him to remind me that he exists. That he cares.

That he is there.

* *

NEIL: John, let me do some of the notes.

JOHN: No chance.

NEIL: Go on.

JOHN: Nah.

NEIL: I'm going out of my mind here, let me do something.

JOHN: Nope.

>*Beat.*

STE: You could clean the van?

NEIL: Nah, I'm alright.

* *

JOHN: A hundred years ago

DOUG: Men our age

STE: Boys

NEIL: Boys our age covered the fields of France

JOHN: They died for honour

STE: To preserve a way of life

NEIL: They died in a fair fight

STE: Watching the enemy

JOHN: Manoeuvring

NEIL: Praying for mistakes

DOUG: Today

NEIL: Those same lads

JOHN: Those same boys who given the chance

DOUG: Would fight for our country

JOHN: Would run into gunfire

STE: Would die to protect our beliefs

NEIL: They're still fighting

DOUG: They're still at war

STE: Only now they battle demons

DOUG: Reflections

JOHN: Social perfections

NEIL: Depressions

DOUG: Ambitions

NEIL: Thoughts

JOHN: The trenches are wrinkles on slowly aging faces

DOUG: No man's land is the image looking back at them from the mirror

STE: There are no rousing speeches

NEIL: No help for heroes

DOUG: But they still battle away

NEIL: Still protecting their honour

STE: Trying to avoid disgrace

JOHN: But this fight isn't fair

NEIL: The opposition is already behind enemy lines

STE: The game is stacked

JOHN: The odds are fixed

DOUG: 100 years ago the biggest killer of young men –

NEIL: Boys

DOUG: 100 years ago it was war

STE: Now they kill themselves.

* *

JOHN: "He went out the usual time. John likes to stick to routines. It was about quarter to 6. I hear him go, but I try to block it out if I'm honest, I know I shouldn't but… He seemed normal. He seemed –"

NEIL: "Neil? He'd been great, really great, looking after me, looking after Emily. Really lovely actually, yeh."

JOHN: "I stayed in bed until about 7, about 7:15. It was a normal day."

NEIL: "I don't think I've told him that though."

DOUG: "Doug –"

NEIL: "I haven't told him enough."

JOHN: "We'd had a lovely weekend."

DOUG: "He works to live."

JOHN: "We had."

DOUG: "He hates work, but you'd never know it at home."

JOHN: "Didn't do anything really."

DOUG: "He's happy here."

JOHN: "Nothing, just lots of very normal, very lovely things."

DOUG: "Always happy, always laughing. Always making me laugh. He can always make me laugh."

STE: "My dad is called Stephen and he works for Network Rail."

DOUG: "He can make anyone laugh, when he's in the mood. Anyone."

STE: "He helps to make sure that the trains run on time."

DOUG: "He gets angry, course, who doesn't, but – he's all hot air."

NEIL: "It had been hard, for both of us."

DOUG: "He'd had a meeting at work on the Monday he told me that. He was worried that he'd got angry. Worried about the consequences."

STE: "He is part of a team who clean the track, the stations and the vehicles to make sure they can continue running."

DOUG: "It's strange because he never normally told me anything about work, so he was obviously –"

JOHN: "He was very concerned."

DOUG: "Upset."

NEIL: "He was scared I think – about money."

STE: "It's a very difficult job, because his team often have to clean up after accidents on the railway."

NEIL: "About his job."

STE: "When I grow up I want to work on the railway as a driver."

JOHN: "John doesn't see himself as others see him. He still saw the kid who failed his exams and left without a chance."

STE: "Dad said, that's where the money is."

DOUG: "He was probably overthinking it."

JOHN: "Where others see warmth and compassion, he sees weaknesses."

NEIL: "I was a month away from statutory pay. It was about to get harder."

STE: "But I don't want to do it because of the money."

JOHN: "He is weak in a way."

STE: "I want to be a driver so that I can drive past him doing his job."

JOHN: "He was fine. He was."

NEIL: "Distant, I remember he was a little distant."

DOUG: "He was, when I think about it, he was irritable."

STE: "And I can sound the horn and wave to him when I see him."

DOUG: "Angry."

NEIL: "Scared."

STE: "And he'll wave back, and he'll know that I'm near him."

JOHN: "Fine."

STE: "I want to work on the railways like my Dad."

* *

JOHN: One for sorrow.

STE: Two for joy.

DOUG: Three for a girl.

NEIL: Four for a boy.

* *

DOUG: Imagine you're on a platform, any platform, they're pretty much universal.

Over here you have your waiting shelter, little bit battered. Maybe a shop here. Benches.

You're under a wooden canopy which runs from the red bricked station building to the platform edge.

Tube lights hanging, some flashing or out. There's lamp posts all the way from one end to the other.

Then there's the platform itself – you normally have an area of tarmac or concrete, or even a mix of the two – maybe crumbling – normally is.

There's a yellow line 1.5 metres from the platform edge. It's on the cusp of where the tarmac meets the tactile paving, you know those little bobbly squares – for blind people.

And then at the edge are these large concrete slabs, massive, they're usually tipped with a faded white line and illustrated with words like "Mind the Gap".

If you jump, this will be the last thing you come into contact with before you hit a train.

The last step you make from this world to the next is from those stones.

Do you know what they are called?

Coping stones. Coping.

They're coping. Copers.

* *

STE: It was a Tuesday

JOHN: The Tuesday after

STE: The Tuesday before

NEIL: Just another day

JOHN: Just another –

DOUG: Tuesday

NEIL: It was cold and frosty

JOHN: Wet and drab

DOUG: I was feeling

NEIL: Overwhelmed

STE: Like I'd been here before

DOUG: Like my mask was cracking

STE: Déjà vu

NEIL: With everything and nothing

DOUG: My defences melting

JOHN: Concerned and confused

NEIL: I'd had an argument

STE: I was hovering above myself, watching

NEIL: And then got a text which said, 'I love you'

DOUG: Like I was weak

JOHN: I couldn't picture the faces

STE: Staring

JOHN: The people I loved

DOUG: That's how it felt

JOHN: Like I was forgetting details

STE: A magpie

NEIL: In the street there was this –

JOHN: Magpie

DOUG: I guess you see signs when you want to don't you

NEIL: My mum had always had this thing with magpies

STE: And my sister

JOHN: They always had this thing

NEIL: Touch black take it back

STE: Touch white make it right

DOUG: Sign of the cross

JOHN: Bow to the bird

STE: If two of you see it, then it's ok, but if you see one on your own, you have to go through this, every time

JOHN: I know it's bullshit

NEIL: But that day, Tuesday

JOHN: I see one, a magpie

DOUG: And I'm walking on my own, and I'm racking my brains for their system

JOHN: Not to do it just to remember it, only, I can't remember it

NEIL: I can't think

STE: And I can see one, a magpie

JOHN: Just on the other side of the road

STE: I'm walking –

JOHN: Because the car's buggered

NEIL: Because of the argument

DOUG: Just to clear my head

STE: And the thing is – it's not just a magpie –

NEIL: It's dying

DOUG: It's a dying magpie

NEIL: One dying magpie

JOHN: One for sorrow.

STE: Two for joy.

DOUG: Three for a girl.

NEIL: Four for a boy.

DOUG: It's been hit by a car or a –

STE: It's been hit by something and it's lay at the side of the road

DOUG: And it's twitching

STE: Just twitching

NEIL: Raising its wings then letting them sag

STE: As if it is trying to feel the wind in them one more time

DOUG: And I think

STE: Not only am I seeing one magpie, on my own, but this is a dying magpie

JOHN: The last thing it will see is me

NEIL: There are omens

JOHN: And then there's this

DOUG: But I don't believe it

STE: So it doesn't matter

NEIL: It doesn't count

STE: Only... I noticed it

JOHN: One, one for sorrow

STE: I noticed it

DOUG: And that is something in itself.

* *

JOHN: You alright?

DOUG: Am I

STE: Alright?

NEIL: Yeh

STE: I need to talk

NEIL: Mate

JOHN: Can I talk?

NEIL: Could we –

DOUG: Would you mind?

NEIL: Get a drink?

JOHN: I need to talk

STE: I need

NEIL: To talk

STE: To someone

JOHN: Anyone

DOUG: Advice

NEIL: I need

JOHN: Just a little

STE: Would you mind?

NEIL: No

DOUG: I never asked

STE: I never said

JOHN: Not their problem

NEIL: It's mine

JOHN: Gasping

STE: Screaming

NEIL: Panting

DOUG: Breath

STE: I'm screaming

JOHN: Help

STE: Help me

DOUG: Help me, please

JOHN: Silence

NEIL: Buzzing

JOHN: Silent

DOUG: But buzzing

NEIL: Ambient

STE: Screeching

JOHN: Quiet

STE: Wailing

DOUG: Whispers

JOHN: Nothing

STE: No one

DOUG: Just whispers

STE: I can't –

JOHN: It's like I'm lost

DOUG: Yeh

STE: It's like I'm lost

JOHN: Lost

STE: But know the way

NEIL: Help

JOHN: Help me – please

NEIL: Like I've been here

DOUG: Seen here

NEIL: Before

JOHN: Like I'm remembering

DOUG: Screaming

STE: But silent

JOHN: Shouting

NEIL: Bawling

JOHN: Hear me

STE: Ask me

JOHN: Hear me

DOUG: Please

STE: Ask me

NEIL: Anyone

JOHN: Someone

STE: No

DOUG: Please

JOHN: No

DOUG: Please

STE: No

JOHN: Gasping

STE: Breathing

NEIL: Panting

DOUG: Breath

JOHN: Gasping

STE: Breathing

NEIL: Panting

DOUG: Breath

JOHN: Air

STE: I need –

JOHN: Gasping

STE: Breathing

NEIL: Panting

DOUG: Breath

JOHN: Air

STE: I need air

NEIL: I need

DOUG: Need air

JOHN: Gasping

STE: Breathing

NEIL: Panting

DOUG: Breath

JOHN: Air

DOUG: I Need. I –

STE: I

NEIL: Need air.

* *

A: Lights.

    Lights curved over the horizon.

    They curved.

    Three lights.

    Strong. White.

    There is speed.

    I am aware of it, though it can't be measured.

    I am aware of – speed.

    I hear the screeching of the tracks, rumbling.

    Metal wheels meet metal track and they screech.

    They shout.

    Scream.

B: He arrived first that day

D: That Tuesday

B: Got into the van, started the engine and put the heaters on full blast

D: He sat there watching as the air chiselled away the condensation

C: He switched the radio on, just to hear other voices

B: But he couldn't focus, it was just noise, so he snapped it off again

D: Panicked, he was panicking

C: He sucked in a deep breath – there was no air

B: Gasping

C: Breathing

D: Panting

A: Weight.

    Moving towards you.

    Arriving.

    It has potential.

D: He exploded from the van

B: The cold air washed over him

C: He ate it

B: Starving

A: I'm aware of colours I've never seen.

    Sounds I'd never heard.

    I've never been more alive.

    More aware.

C: Safety boots

B: Steel toe-caps

C: Steel mid-soles

D: High vis vest

B: Hard hat

A: I feel the ground beneath my feet.

    Concrete.

    Anchoring.

    My legs are heavy.

    Rooted.

D: Clear the obvious

B: The visible

C: The obviously visible

A: I look around.

    No one.

Nothing.

D: The limbs

B: The bones

D: The bodies and the phones

A: Adrenaline pumping.

I'm alive.

C: A Tuesday

B: The Tuesday after

D: The Tuesday before

A: I feel the cold on the tips of my fingers.

The wind in each strand of hair.

B: He never asked

C: He never said

D: Are you alright?

A: An impulse.

A moment.

A heartbeat.

A –

Train noise builds to a crescendo.

Lights.

WWW.OBERONBOOKS.COM